Fr. P

Consecration Sunday Stewardship Program

Herb Miller

Abingdon Press
Nashville

Consecration Sunday Stewardship Program

Herb Miller

About the Author

Herb Miller is executive director of the Net Results Resources Center, Lubbock, Texas ; and succeeded Lyle E. Schaller as parish consultant for the Yokefellow Institute, Richmond, Indiana.

01 02 03 04—10 9 8 7

Printed in the United States of America

CONTENTS

WARNING!

Churches should not try to save money by doing the program without an outside leader. That is quite expensive in several ways. First, it reduces success by 10.0 percent to 15.0 percent. Thus, churches with a $100,000 annual budget will get $10,000 to $15,000 less than they would with an outside leader.

Second, having done the program wrong the first time, they will repeat their mistake in the future, compounding their cost into astronomical figures and blocking many members from the spiritual growth which would have come from tithing and percentage giving.

An outside leader is an absolute necessity because

A. People and pastor work harder.

B. An outside leader takes a fresh approach, thus causing more attention and serious concentration on the subject.

C. Committee members are far less likely to take shortcuts which reduce final results. The outside authority figure allows a pastor to suggest that "we telephone and check with the leader before we make a change in the program."

D. An outside leader will make at least a 10.0 percent difference in the total results.

For the Pastor and Key Leaders: Guidelines for Obtaining an Outside Leader

Selecting and scheduling outside leaders is totally in the hands of local congregations. Abingdon Press and the Net Results Resource Center do not maintain lists of outside leaders for Consecration Sunday for various parts of the country, do not deploy outside leaders to congregations, are in no way involved

4

in setting honoraria for the outside leaders, and receive no portion of the honoraria that congregations pay outside leaders. Select a pastor or lay leader in whom you have confidence. Someone who has no experience whatever with Consecration Sunday, provided that person has good public-speaking ability, can be just as effective the first time he or she serves as an outside leader for Consecration Sunday as he or she will be the tenth time around the track. If a congregation's leaders do not know someone who already has experience as an outside leader, they should select a person they respect as a speaker. That is often a judicatory staff person, such as district superintendent, who has Sundays available. Sometimes, a retired pastor can fill this role. In some settings, two pastors can lead Consecration Sunday in each other's congregations.

Give the outside leader three resources. Suggest that in preparation for the role, he or she should, in the following order, (1) listen to the audiotape, (2) read the program book, and (3) read the leader's guide. After reviewing these resources, if the outside leader has questions, he or she may fax Herb Miller at 806/798-2021 (his constant travel makes phone calls impossible). Rarely, however, are such fax communications necessary. The materials are quite self-explanatory.

Congregational leaders should set the honorarium at a level consistent with what is customary for guest speakers in their part of the country. In addition to the honorarium, they should also pay the outside leader appropriate travel expenses for the three trips.

Consecration Sunday

GENERAL INFORMATION FOR LEADERS

Our stewardship education emphasis this year will culminate with a Consecration Sunday. During the morning worship service on that day, members of the congregation will make their financial commitments to the church's work in the community and its missionary, benevolent, and educational programs around the world.

I. Philosophy of Consecration Sunday

Two general methods are used to secure money for churches. One is the "begging" method. This is the age-old plan of going door-to-door to present the "needs of the church" as outlined in a budget. The second and more appropriate method is education. Recognizing that most Christians are victims of bad giving habits, our stewardship program this year is an organized, intensive effort to teach the members of our congregation the principles of Christian stewardship. Consecration Sunday is based on the philosophy of "the need of the giver to give" for his or her own spiritual development, rather than on the "need of the church to receive." Instead of treating people like members of a social club who need to pay dues, we will be treating people like followers of Jesus Christ who want to give unselfishly as an act of discipleship.

II. The Goal of Consecration Sunday

Our goal is to raise the level of giving of individuals to the church, rather than to raise a church budget. Church budgets usually reflect the minimum needs of the church and, therefore, often pull down the level of giving instead of raising it. Our task this year is to make good stewards; to teach people to accept a sacred partnership with God; to combat the sin of covetousness by accepting the Bible's standard of good giving, the tithe; and to encourage people to give proportionately and systematically in keeping with their ability.

III. The Plan for Consecration Sunday

There will be no tricks. Every member who makes a pledge will do so by voluntarily coming to the church on Consecration Sunday for the purpose of making his or her financial commitment to the Lord's work and eating a Celebration Luncheon together. Even those who have strong personal opposition to signing pledge cards are urged to attend. The program is done in such a way that there will be no personal embarrassment if people do not choose to fill out an Estimate of Giving Card. This plan represents a great faith in our people. There will be no home solicitation of pledges. At the morning worship service, the guest leader will conduct a period of instruction and inspiration, climaxed by members making their own commitment as an act of worship. Each person will fill in his/her own commitment card, and no member will solicit another member. The commitment will be strictly between each member, God, and the financial secretary. The commitment period will begin with the start of the new church year and will continue until further notice.

IV. The Organization for Consecration Sunday

Obtaining participation in Consecration Sunday events will be accomplished through the Consecration Sunday committee and church board members. Someone will be responsible to see that every member of the church participates in two events: (1) morning worship on Consecration Sunday and (2) the Celebration Luncheon immediately following worship that same day.

V. The Key to Success

The individual responsibility level of each Consecration Sunday committee member and board member is crucial. The program rides or fails with them. Since there will be no follow-up calls, every effort must be made to inform, inspire, and commit every church member to attend the two events.

Time Line

Approximately six weeks prior to Consecration Sunday:
The outside leader meets for one hour with the Consecration
Sunday committee. *Do not attempt to do this program without an
outside leader. The results will be drastically reduced if you do so.* The
outside leader will need to visit the church a total of three
times—once for this first meeting, once for the parish board dinner on Sunday or Monday before Consecration Sunday, and
once for the Sunday morning worship service and Celebration
Luncheon. Each of these is important. To eliminate the outside
leader from any of the visits will appreciably reduce the results.

**Sunday, _____ (three weeks before Consecra-
tion Sunday):** A committee member makes a brief announcement in adult Sunday school classes and morning worship
regarding importance of the Consecration Sunday and Celebration Luncheon on _____, _____
(day and date). *Do not* stress the need of the church for funds.
Stress the need of the giver to give a tithe or a specific percentage
of his or her income as a part of his or her commitment to Jesus
Christ and spiritual development. Stress the fact that the Celebration Luncheon will be a catered meal, *not* a potluck dinner.

**Monday, _____ (three weeks before Consecra-
tion Sunday):** Mail Letter #1 (see model on following pages).

**Sunday, _____ (two weeks before Consecra-
tion Sunday):** A *different* committee member makes a brief
announcement in adult Sunday school classes and morning
worship regarding importance of the Consecration Sunday and
Celebration Luncheon on _____,
_____ (day and date). *Do not* stress the need of
the church for funds. Stress the need of the giver to give a tithe
or a specific percentage of his or her income as a part of his or
her commitment to Jesus Christ and spiritual development.
Stress the fact that the Celebration Luncheon will be a catered
meal, *not* a potluck dinner.

Monday, _____ (two weeks before Consecration Sunday): Mail Letter #2 (see model on following pages).

Tuesday and Wednesday, _____ (two weeks before Consecration Sunday): Parish board dinner telephone chair (someone who will be pleasant and thorough in making all contacts) phones all parish board members and their spouses and all Consecration Sunday committee members and spouses, stressing the importance of their attendance at a dinner for church leaders at _____ p.m., _____, _____ (day and date) at a restaurant (not at the church), at which time _____ (an outside leader) will speak to them about the upcoming Consecration Sunday and the spiritual dimensions of stewardship.

Sunday, _____ (one week before Consecration Sunday): A *different* committee member uses the "Grow One Step" sheet in morning worship. Distribute copies by placing one in each worship bulletin. Start with the stair-steps side of the sheet. *Do not* print the figures from your church on the sheet. Rather, the committee member asks worship attenders to write in the blanks the figures he or she reads from the pulpit. Start on the bottom of the stair steps and read the figures for worship attenders to write in. As the committee member gives each figure, he or she should give an illustration of what this means. Examples: $.01 to $4.99 per week equals a movie or lunch; $5.00 to $9.99 equals one golf game; $10.00 to $14.99 equals getting your hair done; $15.00 to $19.99 equals taking your family to lunch. Next, ask people to look at the chart on the back of the "Grow One Step" sheet and let their eyes go down the left side of the scale until they come to their salary level—then ask them to move their eyes across to their weekly giving level—then move their eyes up to what percentage that is of their income. Ask them to be thinking and praying this week about what percentage of their income God is calling them to give.

Ask worship service and Sunday school attenders to make reservations to attend morning worship and the Celebration Luncheon next Sunday, _____ (Consecration Sunday date). Tell them that we will be making home visits to persons from whom we do not receive a luncheon reservation card, so it is very important that everyone who is present this morning turn in a luncheon reservation card. In order to get these luncheon reservation cards filled out, the pastor should say something like the following: "The ushers are now going to pass each of you a card. We will give you five minutes to fill these out; then the ushers will come back to take them up again." (See the model card provided for this purpose.) Do not place the cards in the bulletin. Do not place them in the pew racks. Do not ask people to place them in the offering plates. All these methods sharply reduce the number of cards which will be turned in. You may want to have some special background music while people are completing the cards.

Sunday, _____ (one week before Consecration Sunday): The pastor preaches on Christian stewardship, emphasizing tithing and percentage giving (the need for a decision to start somewhere, whether 5 percent or 6 percent or 7 percent)— not as a legalistic rule but as a response to God's love for us.

_____ p.m., _____ (one hour before the church leader dinner held on Sunday or Monday evening of the week before Consecration Sunday): The outside leader meets at the church with the pastor, financial secretary, and Consecration Sunday committee members. This checkup meeting finalizes plans for Consecration Sunday, especially at the point of organizing to obtain luncheon reservations from persons who have not yet made them.

_____ p.m., _____ (Sunday or Monday evening of the week before Consecration Sunday): The outside leader speaks at a dinner for church leaders at a local restaurant. This includes key elected church leaders (like elders, deacons, and deaconesses), financial secretary, members of the Consecration Sunday committee, and the spouses of persons in each of these groups. At the close of this meeting, distribute and read aloud a copy of the sheet entitled "Instructions for Making Celebration Luncheon Reservation Contacts." Then, make assignments for Consecration Sunday Reservation Card visits to all church members and "friends of the church" not present for morning worship today or this special dinner (keep a record of which leaders take which member names for contact). Do this by having the pastor or Consecration Sunday chair call out the names of these families as church leaders raise their hands and volunteer to call on them for the purpose of obtaining their reservations for the catered Celebration Luncheon on Consecration Sunday, _____ (date). In larger churches, lay the cards on a table in alphabetical order to be picked up (recording on a master sheet who takes which cards). Ask that these contacts be made Tuesday and Wednesday evening.

Monday, _____ (the week before Consecration Sunday): Mail Letter #3 (see model on following pages).

Tuesday and Wednesday, _____ (the week before Consecration Sunday): Personal visits are made by church officers and Consecration Sunday committee members to obtain Celebration Luncheon reservations from members who have not yet made them.

Thursday, _____ (by 7:00 p.m.): All Celebration Luncheon reservations from personal contacts by church officers and Consecration Sunday committee members are phoned in to the Consecration Sunday committee chair.

Thursday, _____ (after 7:00 p.m.): The Consecration Sunday chair telephones all church officers and Consecration Sunday committee members who have *not* turned their cards in and asks for their reports. If they have not finished their contacts, he asks for them to be completed this evening and be phoned in by 9:30 p.m.

Friday, _____ (after 7:00 p.m., the week before Consecration Sunday): The Consecration Sunday committee chair telephones for reservations of any members or "friends of the church" who did not get contacted by the church officers or Consecration Sunday committee members.

Sunday, _____ (Consecration Sunday): The outside leader preaches in morning worship and conducts a commitment session at the close of the service. Time length of other parts of the service should be kept as brief as possible so as to allow for this closing part. Do *not* plan to use a choral response of any kind at the end of the service. The printed order of worship should conclude with "Commitment Time and Benediction. . . . . Name of Outside Leader."

Immediately after worship, the financial secretary and an assistant should be prepared to use an adding machine in the church office to tally all pledges so as to produce a report in a few minutes for presentation at the conclusion of the Celebration Luncheon. He/she will already have totaled the giving figure records from each family unit from the previous twelve-month period and have these ready for use in preparing the various percentages and totals needed for the Comprehensive Statistical Report on Consecration Sunday Results (to be completed by financial secretary—see model form). This report form will be brought to the concluding part of the Celebration Luncheon for announcement at the appropriate time by the Consecration Sunday committee chair. After this report is given, the Doxology should be sung as a conclusion to the celebration.

Monday, _____ (the day after Consecration Sunday): Mail Letter #4 (see model on following pages) to persons who did not *attend* the Consecration Sunday service yesterday. Include a stamped, addressed, return envelope and an Estimate of Giving Card. Type on the card the name and address of the person receiving the letter. This personalizing of the card greatly increases the return rate.

Monday _____ (one week after Consecration Sunday): Mail a personalized letter of appreciation to each of the individuals or families who filled out an Estimate of Giving Card. The letter should state the exact dollar amount of their commitment.

Final Word

If you follow the above instructions to the letter, everybody wins: The church wins! You win! God wins! Congratulations!

Letters, Estimate of Giving Cards, and Posters

Letter #1
(To be mailed to all members and friends of the church)

[Date--Monday, three weeks before Consecration Sunday]

Dear Members and Friends of _____ Church:

Sunday, _____, will be Consecration Sunday at
_____ Church. I urge you to plan now to attend
the two important events of this day: first, the Sunday morning
worship service and, second, the Celebration Luncheon immediately after worship that same day (a special catered meal, *not*
a potluck dinner).

This will be a biblical, spiritual, inspirational program
designed to enrich our understanding of Christian stewardship.
The program is not built on the "need of the church to receive,"
but on the "need of the giver to give" as a part of his or her own
spiritual development and Christian commitment.

We believe that you are concerned enough to come to the
church on Consecration Sunday to make your financial commitment as an act of worship in the church sanctuary. ~~This means
that no one will call on you at your home for a pledge.~~ But you will
be contacted personally to secure your commitment to attend
morning worship on Consecration Sunday and the Celebration
Luncheon immediately after worship.

Cordially,

Board Chairperson

ENCLOSED PLEASE FIND
A RESERVATION FOR
THE CONSECRATION SUNDAY
LUNCHEON. PLEASE LET
US KNOW OF YOUR
ATTENDANCE

13

Letter #2
(To be mailed to all church officers and Consecration Sunday
committee members)

[Date--Monday, two weeks before Consecration Sunday]

TO: Church Officers and Consecration Sunday Committee
Members
[List the individual names in a vertical column and place a
red check mark by the name of each individual to whom the
letter is mailed.]

Ladies and Gentlemen:

I need your help in order to make our Consecration Sunday
a success. You will *not* be asked to call in homes to obtain
pledges from people. But there are other ways in which your
assistance is essential.

We are asking that you be our guests for a dinner at ___ p.m.
_____, _____ (Sunday or Monday of
the week prior to Consecration Sunday), at _____
(a local restaurant—not at the church). _____
(name of outside leader) will bring a brief message, in which he
or she will talk about the spiritual dimensions of stewardship in
preparation for our Consecration Sunday.

Your attendance will strengthen the success of our stewardship emphasis and, thereby, our whole church program for the
coming year.

Sincerely,

Consecration Sunday Chairperson

Letter #3

(To be mailed to all members and friends of the church)

[Date--the Monday before Consecration Sunday]

Dear Members and Friends of _____
Church:

You are, by now, surely aware that Sunday,
_____, is Consecration Sunday at our church.

We believe that you have enough concern for your church to attend the two special events of this day: first, the Sunday morning worship service and, second, the Celebration Luncheon immediately following worship.

This will be a catered meal, so we need to take reservations for each person who will be present. If you have not made plans to attend these two events, please do so. Our goal is to have every member and friend of the church present. If you did not make a reservation last Sunday, please let us know you will be present for the two events by calling _____ (Consecration Sunday chair) at _____ (phone number).

Remember that the success of our church programming next year depends on your initiative and dedication. We are asking each individual to make whatever sacrifices are necessary in order to be present on _____ (date).

Your servant in Christ,

Pastor

Letter #4

(To be mailed to all persons who did not attend Consecration Sunday services. Be certain not to send this letter to those who attended the services, but decided not to complete an Estimate of Giving Card.)

[Date--Monday after Consecration Sunday]

Dear Christian Friends:

We had a great crowd and excellent response for our Consecration Sunday yesterday. We are sorry that you could not be with us, but we know you will wish to participate in the financial support of your church during the coming year. We have, therefore, enclosed your Estimate of Giving Card. Could you help us to complete the campaign by returning it this week?

We appreciate your help in bringing this fine campaign to a good conclusion.

Sincerely,

Consecration Sunday Chairperson

[Note: It is important that the Estimate of Giving Card enclosed with this letter have the names and addresses already typed on it. This will greatly increase the return rate.]

Letter #5

One week after Consecration Sunday, mail a personalized letter of appreciation to each individual or family who filled out an Estimate of Giving card. The letter should state the exact dollar amount of their commitment.

Estimate of Giving Cards

Obtain these cards from the bookstore or church supply catalog from which you bought the program, or from Cokesbury 800/672-1789 or 615/749-6113. Under no circumstances should the cards be mailed or distributed in advance of Consecration Sunday or prior to the end of the service. It is wisest for the guest leader to bring the cards with him/her on Consecration Sunday.

Posters

Make some big signs to place around the church which say "It's Coming: _____ (date)."

Instructions for Making Celebration Luncheon Reservation Contacts

Permission is hereby granted to photocopy this page for use with the "Consecration Sunday Stewardship Program."

I. Our goal is to secure a promise from every church member to participate in Consecration Sunday by attending

    A. morning service on Consecration Sunday, _____ (date).

    B. the Celebration Luncheon immediately following worship that same day.

II. The visitor's job is to get the member or "friend of the church" to attend. This task does not include securing a pledge, nor should visitors be concerned about the amount to which the person may commit.

III. Attendance at the two events is accomplished by the following steps:

    A. Each visitor is to make a personal contact with every person on his or her list _____ and _____ (the Tuesday and Wednesday prior to Consecration Sunday). It is too easy to ignore or "forget" a telephone call or to say "no" to the appeal. This call in the home should seek to inform people of the total Consecration Sunday plan.

    B. Emphasize the voluntary aspect of coming to the church for the morning worship and Celebration Luncheon on Sunday, _____ (date). Stress the fact that no one will solicit their pledge, but that their decision will be made in privacy as an act of worship—between the person and God. Use the reservation card to make their reservation for the two events.

IV. Make a full report of the results of your contacts to the Consecration Sunday chair by 7:00 p.m., _____, the Wednesday (Thursday evening if the church leader dinner was on Monday) before Consecration Sunday.

Consecration Sunday Reservation Card

I will be present for Morning Worship and the Celebration Luncheon on Sunday, _____ (date).

_____ yes _____ no

The number of persons attending from my family will be _____.

Name _____

Phone _____

Comprehensive Statistical Report on Consecration Sunday Results

(To be completed by financial secretary)

A total of _____ giving units (husbands and wives or single persons) completed Estimate of Giving Cards this year.

A total of _____ of these giving units increased their financial commitment above their last year's amount.

A total of _____ giving units present to fill out commitment cards today committed a total of $_____. Based on last year's giving records, $_____ can be expected for the coming year from persons who have established giving patterns but are *not* present today. This gives us a grand total of $_____ in anticipated income for the next twelve months.

Total income of the general budget during the last twelve months was $_____. Next year, our income can be expected to increase by $_____. This is a _____ percent increase in total giving above last year.

Permission is hereby granted to photocopy this page for use with the "Consecration Sunday Stewardship Program."

Responsibility List for Consecration Sunday

1. Consecration Sunday Chair

2. Celebration Luncheon Chair

3. Parish Board Dinner Telephone Chair

4. Person to make morning worship and Sunday church school announcement three weeks before Consecration Sunday.

5. Person to make morning worship and Sunday church school announcement two weeks before Consecration Sunday.

6. Person to present "Grow One Step" sheet one week before Consecration Sunday in morning worship.

7. Financial Secretary to make advance computations in preparation for making final calculations right after worship on Consecration Sunday, so that the total of the pledges can be announced by the time people finish eating. She or he should obtain an assistant for Consecration Sunday morning, so that this can be rapidly accomplished.

Answers to Questions Often Asked about the *Consecration Sunday* Stewardship Program

1. How do we handle the meal when we have more than one worship service?

If your church is in a small town, you have two worship services, and attendance at the first service is sparse, most of the first-service attenders are willing to return for a noon meal.

If your church is in a metropolitan area where many of the first-service attenders drive a great distance, schedule a brunch after the first service and a luncheon after the second service.

If you have two, three, or four morning worship services, schedule a brunch after each service.

One Roman Catholic church scheduled and took reservations for six dessert fellowships following six masses from Saturday through Sunday evening.

If you elect to schedule two or more brunches, either report the results from each worship service at each brunch, or wait until next Sunday to report the results, or report the results in next week's newsletter and morning worship bulletin.

2. Are you sure we must have a *catered* meal?

The meal must not be a standard fellowship dinner to which everyone brings food, because that eliminates the need to secure reservations for the meal. Removing the reservation procedure significantly reduces the sizable crowd that always results from that procedure, thus eliminating a great part of the positive result. Successful alternatives have, however, included the following:

- In one church, a member who was a professional caterer prepared the meal at a reduced price.

- In another church, the women's organization from a neighboring congregation prepared the meal at a reduced price.

- In another congregation, a man responsible for the annual community barbecue took charge of preparing the meal, got a rancher to donate a steer, and catered a barbecue luncheon at a reduced cost.

- Because they recognize that it is crucial to the effectiveness of Consecration Sunday, one or more individuals sometimes volunteer to donate all or most of the meal cost.

3. Can we change the Estimate of Giving card to allow a blank for designated gifts or to stamp identifying information about our church? Can we use another type of card? Can we have it printed or photocopied ourselves instead of buying it from you? Can we reword it so it doesn't emphasize the word *tithe* so much?

The Estimate of Giving card is copyrighted, and permission to change the wording is *never* granted. No valid reasons exist for adding to or changing the wording of the card, which has worked well in thousands of churches of every size and denomination for more than a dozen years.

You cannot design a card that will precisely satisfy every individual who completes one. Experience indicates that if people prefer to state that their giving will be monthly, rather than weekly as the card indicates, they will cross out *weekly* and write *monthly*. Or, if they prefer to write *quarterly*, they will do that.

Redesigning the card for multiple purposes, such as designated gifts or building-fund use, is never advisable. Other kinds of campaigns should be done separately, at a different time on the calendar. If your church's long-term tradition necessitates a designation of money for two or more funds, the guest leader can mention this orally—at the time the cards are distributed on Consecration Sunday morning—asking people to note on their cards a division of the total into those categories, if they wish to do so.

While the card, in and of itself, is not the only reason Consecration Sunday succeeds, why run the risk of altering the card when experience has indicated that such changes are neither necessary nor advisable?

4. We have a problem with the idea of people signing their cards—if this is truly a matter between them and God.

Research shows that people who complete cards but do not sign them give an average of 30 percent less than those who do. As with most other spiritual matters, commitments are inevitably stronger when people do not keep them totally secret. If we are going to put the effort into conducting a Consecration Sunday Stewardship Program, why risk compromising the result in such a major way?

5. Must we have a nice dinner for the leaders on the Sunday or Monday prior to Consecration Sunday, or can a group in the church fix it, or can it be potluck?

Scheduling the dinner for the leaders at a local restaurant is the best approach. However, large congregations that regularly provide good food through a catering service or by church employees can schedule this leaders' meal at the church. Unlike the Consecration Sunday Celebration Luncheon, if the leaders pay for this meal, it will not damage the final financial results (although this is *not* the preferred approach). The leaders' meal must *not*, however, be a potluck or one that involves members in preparing the food.

6. Can we take donations or in another way have the meals (the Celebration Luncheon and/or the leaders' dinner) paid for?

Do not take donations for the Consecration Sunday meal. Take the money from the budget. Sometimes, however, one or more key leaders will decide to donate the meal cost the first year, in order to get the process started. (By contrast, you *can* allow the leaders to pay for their meals at the leaders' dinner the previous Sunday or Monday, if your committee strongly prefers to do it that way.)

7. Does the guest leader have to be present for all three events? (Sometimes the church has already obtained or wants to obtain a specific leader, then finds out he/she is not available for all the specified times.)

The best results are attained when the guest leader is present on all three occasions called for in the program outline. If this is not possible, his or her absence from the initial setup meeting six weeks or more ahead of Consecration Sunday does the least damage to the final financial outcome. His or her presence at the leaders' dinner and the Consecration Sunday worship service is essential to positive end results.

8. How do we most accurately compare the financial figures? (We may have designated funds, wonder how to include older children of members, or have had some anomaly in our budget during the previous 12 months such as losing some big givers.)

Use the instruction sheet provided in the Consecration Sunday material. Focus on operational budget giving. Do not include designated giving in these totals, since they are not the objective of the Consecration Sunday program. However, if your church traditionally uses two-envelope or three-envelope commitment cards, you should include the *total* giving pattern, not just the operational gift.

If one or more large givers from last year is no longer present in the church, you may want to identify that in your report as a footnote by saying something like, "We have achieved these results despite the fact that several major donors from last year have moved away or are now deceased." This puts the results into a rational perspective.

9. We have difficulty with the philosophy of using the "Grow 1 Step" page—people feel uncomfortable and perhaps they will be resentful with being "labeled" publicly regarding how their giving compares to other members.

No church, among the thousands that have used this procedure, has reported such a response. Curiosity, interest, and personal reflection on the spiritual aspects of financial giving are the primary results of using the "Grow 1 Step" sheet.

10. We've never had a pledge drive before, and people are struggling with the concept of even pledging.

Research indicates that people who write their financial stewardship intentions on a card during annual programs of this sort give an average of two times as much as people who do not fill out such cards. Very few people respond negatively to this procedure. The guest leader makes it clear that completing the card is not mandatory, and persons who prefer not to do so will not be publicly embarrassed by that decision. Experience indicates that a majority of people who do not fill out a card the first year their church uses Consecration Sunday will decide to do so the second year.

11. We have heard how successful Consecration Sunday has been in other churches, and we want to know if we can use it for other purposes, like making up for a budget shortfall this year (as a result of a poor pledge drive last year) or a capital "one time" drive for something like debt retirement or a new building.

Do not use Consecration Sunday for any purpose than an annual operating campaign. It works extremely well for that purpose and that purpose only.

12. Where is a list of each of the committee member's responsibilities? (The committee members are listed on one page and their responsibilities are listed as they fall in the time line.)

In the meeting with the outside leader six weeks before Consecration Sunday, the group goes through the time line together. Each leader checks items that are his or her responsibility. This is the best approach for learning how the parts of the time line fit together and learning how each leader's role interconnects with the roles of other leaders.

13. Do you recommend outside leaders? Do you keep lists of churches of our denomination that have done the program, so that we can speak to the pastors?

We do not keep such lists, which would number in the thousands. Someone at your regional denominational office may know of congregations in your area that have used Consecration Sunday. Those churches could give you names of outside leaders. However, the person you select does not have to have previously led a Consecration Sunday in order to get good results. Follow the guest leader selection suggestions in the

Consecration Sunday booklet and ask him or her to carefully study the instructions in the guest leader guide.

14. Can we photocopy parts of the program book (or leader's guide)?

Only those pages where permission is given to photocopy. These are copyrighted materials, protected by U.S. and international copyright laws. These materials are quite inexpensive, and their cost will not prevent congregations of any size from using the program.

15. Do you have suggestions for the stewardship sermon the pastor gives the week before?

Obtain a copy of *Money Isn't Is Everything* by Herb Miller or *Right On the Money* by Brian Bauknight. Both books are published in Nashville by Discipleship Resources (phone 800-685-4370 or 404/442-8761).

16. We've done Consecration Sunday two/three years and had good results. Should we go on using it?

Some churches report good results the fourth and fifth years—contrary to experiences with other kinds of stewardship programs. Take great care, however, not to modify or leave out some of the parts, as that reduces results. However we do not recommend your using any stewardship program for more than three years in a row. When you decide to shift to another program, use a program that uses a similar philosophical and theological base.

17. We want to do a stewardship emphasis on time and talents as well. Can we do this at the same time as Consecration Sunday?

Don't! Research indicates that doing them together reduces results on both sides of the equation. If you do that, some peoplc will inevitably say, "I can't give money, but I can give time." This is not a multiple-choice question. Putting it in that way is neither biblical nor effective. Use a "Spiritual Gifts Emphasis Month" fourteen to thirty days earlier or later than Consecration Sunday. Procedures for accomplishing that are found in the *Net Results* reprint pac titled *Involving Members/Attenders in Ministries*. Obtain from *Net Results*, 5001 Avenue N, Lubbock, TX 79412-2993; phone 806/762-8094.

18. We are having a special Sunday coming up about the same time as we usually do our pledge Sunday (e.g., our church's centennial). Can we combine this with Consecration Sunday?

Don't do it! You will reduce the effectiveness of both.

19. Can you do Consecration Sunday and then at another point in the year do a capital-funds campaign?

Yes. Try to keep them separate by about four months.

20. Do we have to make home visits or can we make phone calls to get the reservations?

Home visits work best. Urge your people to do it that way. Be aware, however, that some will phone instead. This will not destroy the program's results.

21. Are you sure we shouldn't do more follow-up to get the remaining cards completed?

Absolutely sure! You said in the publicity that you wouldn't do this. If you do, people will not believe you next year. Experience indicates that such contacts (instead of the recommended letter on the Monday following Consecration Sunday) do not increase the actual amount of dollars given that year by more than 1 percent. You are much better off, long term, when you help people develop the habit of bringing their offerings to God's house, instead of chasing them down.

22. We are afraid of the "leap of faith" of not putting the budget together and letting everyone know the amount needed (or we struggle with the logistics of our committees' not being able to do the advance planning on their budgets as they are used to).

After you have done it this way once, you will never go back to setting the budget first—because you will see the enormous increase in giving that occurs when people give to God as part of their spiritual growth rather than giving to the budget. Church budgets put a ceiling on giving, above which the total offerings seldom rise. The committees can, of course, begin to do some individual planning at the same time they have usually done that in past years. Just do *not* put all the figures together into a grand total—until after the Consecration Sunday results are in.

23. How do you decide who should be contacted about this program (i.e., how inactive is inactive)?

Inactive means they have not worshiped in your congregation even once during the past year and have no recorded financial giving during the past year. Most congregations find it best to work on efforts to get such persons reconnected with church participation *before* they ask them for financial donations. This keeps people from saying, "All they are concerned about is my money."

A REVEALING BREAKDOWN OF OUR CONGREGATION'S GIVING PATTERNS

FIND WHERE YOU ARE ON THIS CHART
(your weekly giving)

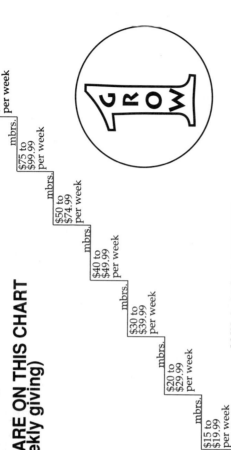

_____ mbrs.
$150 and up per week

_____ mbrs.
$100 to $149.99 per week

_____ mbrs.
$75 to $99.99 per week

_____ mbrs.
$50 to $74.99 per week

_____ mbrs.
$40 to $49.99 per week

_____ mbrs.
$30 to $39.99 per week

_____ mbrs.
$20 to $29.99 per week

_____ mbrs.
$15 to $19.99 per week

_____ mbrs.
$10 to $14.99 per week

_____ mbrs.
$5 to $9.99 per week

_____ mbrs.
1¢ to $4.99 per week

_____ mbrs.
$0

WILL YOU GROW
ONE STEP THIS YEAR?

Permission is hereby granted to photocopy this page for use with the "Consecration Sunday Stewardship Program."

WEEKLY INCOME	BEYOND A TITHE		TITHE	UPPER RANGE GIVING			MIDDLE RANGE GIVING			LOWER RANGE GIVING		
	15%	12%	10%	9%	8%	7%	6%	5%	4%	3%	2%	1%
$ 100.00	15.00	12.00	10.00	9.00	8.00	7.00	6.00	5.00	4.00	3.00	2.00	1.00
$ 200.00	30.00	24.00	20.00	18.00	16.00	14.00	12.00	10.00	8.00	6.00	4.00	2.00
$ 300.00	45.00	36.00	30.00	27.00	24.00	21.00	18.00	15.00	12.00	9.00	6.00	3.00
$ 400.00	60.00	48.00	40.00	36.00	32.00	28.00	24.00	20.00	16.00	12.00	8.00	4.00
$ 500.00	75.00	60.00	50.00	45.00	40.00	35.00	30.00	25.00	20.00	15.00	10.00	5.00
$ 600.00	90.00	72.00	60.00	54.00	48.00	42.00	36.00	30.00	24.00	18.00	12.00	6.00
$ 700.00	105.00	84.00	70.00	63.00	56.00	49.00	42.00	35.00	28.00	21.00	14.00	7.00
$ 800.00	120.00	96.00	80.00	72.00	64.00	56.00	48.00	40.00	32.00	24.00	16.00	8.00
$ 900.00	135.00	108.00	90.00	81.00	72.00	63.00	54.00	45.00	36.00	27.00	18.00	9.00
$1,000.00	150.00	120.00	100.00	90.00	80.00	70.00	60.00	50.00	40.00	30.00	20.00	10.00
$1,100.00	165.00	132.00	110.00	99.00	88.00	77.00	66.00	55.00	44.00	33.00	22.00	11.00
$1,200.00	180.00	144.00	120.00	108.00	96.00	84.00	72.00	60.00	48.00	36.00	24.00	12.00
$2,500.00	375.00	300.00	250.00	225.00	200.00	175.00	150.00	125.00	100.00	75.00	50.00	25.00

1. Find where YOU are on the chart (your weekly income/giving).
2. Move one block to the left to determine what GROW ONE % would be for you.